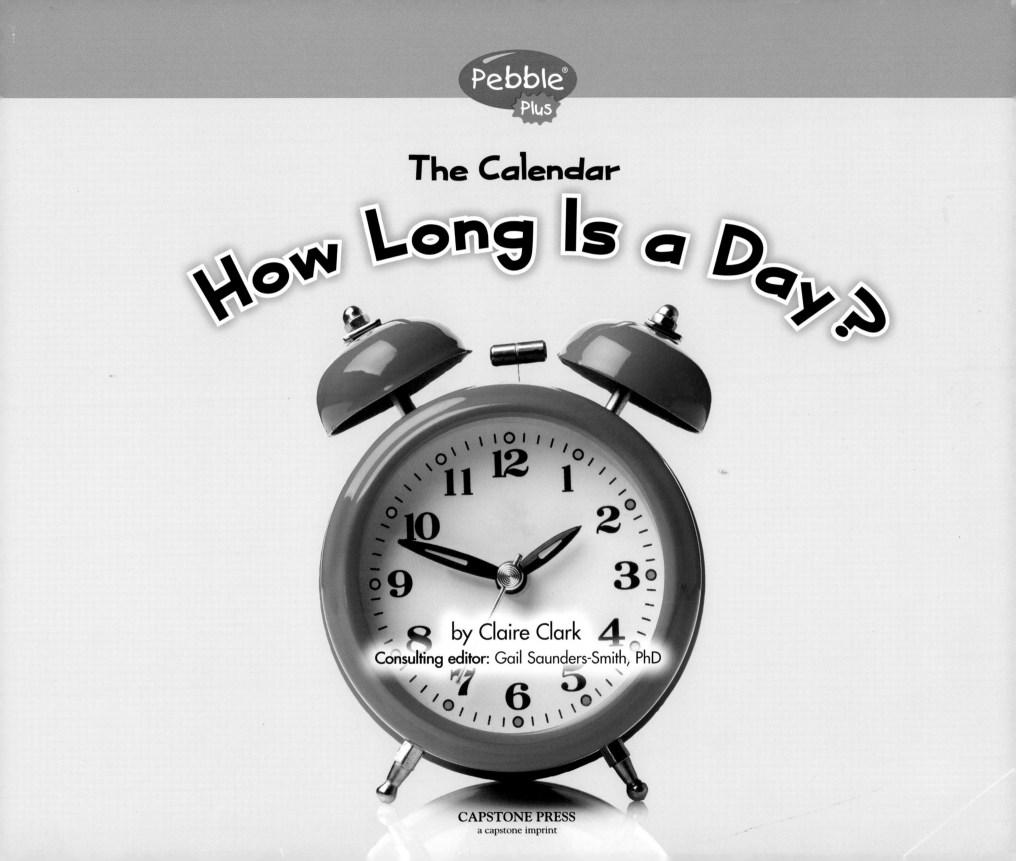

Pebble® Plus

The Calendar

# How Long Is a Day?

by Claire Clark

Consulting editor: Gail Saunders-Smith, PhD

CAPSTONE PRESS

a capstone imprint

Pebble Plus is published by Capstone Press,
1710 Roe Crest Drive, North Mankato, Minnesota 56003.
www.capstonepub.com

Books published by Capstone Press are manufactured with paper
containing at least 10 percent post-consumer waste.

*Library of Congress Cataloging-in-Publication Data*
Clark, Claire, 1973-
  How long is a day? / by Claire Clark.
    p. cm. — (Pebble plus. The calendar)
  Summary: "Simple text and photos explain a day as a unit of time and the parts of a day"—Provided by publisher.
  Includes bibliographical references and index.
  ISBN 978-1-4296-7591-8 (lib. bdg.) —ISBN 978-1-4296-7897-1 (pbk.)
  1. Day—Juvenile literature. 2. Night—Juvenile literature. 3. Earth—Rotation—Juvenile literature. 4. Time
measurements—Juvenile literature.  I. Title.
  QB209.5.C583 2012
  529'.1—dc23
                                                                        2011021344

**Editorial Credits**
Kristen Mohn, editor; Bobbie Nuytten, designer; Marcie Spence, media researcher; Marcy Morin, studio scheduler;
    Kathy McColley, production specialist


**Photo Credits**
Capstone Studio: Karon Dubke, cover (left), 5, 7, 11, 13, 15, 17, 19, 21; Shutterstock: Alex Staroseltsev,
    cover (right), 1, beboy, 9

## Note to Parents and Teachers

The Calendar series supports national science and social studies standards related to time.
This book describes and illustrates what makes a day. The images support early readers in
understanding the text. The repetition of words and phrases helps early readers learn new
words. This book also introduces early readers to subject-specific vocabulary words, which are
defined in the Glossary section. Early readers may need assistance to read some words and to
use the Table of Contents, Glossary, Read More, Internet Sites, and Index sections of the book.

Printed in the United States of America in North Mankato, Minnesota.
102011      006405CGS12

# Table of Contents

# What Is a Day?

Guess what happened

while you were sleeping?

A new day began!

Each new day begins at midnight.

A day lasts 24 hours.

Seven days are in a week.
A year is made up of
365 days. A calendar shows
all the days in a year.

# What Makes a Day?

Earth spins like a top.

In 24 hours Earth spins

completely around one time.

One spin is one day.

Spinning gives us day
and night. As Earth spins,
the part facing the sun
has daylight. The part
facing away is dark.

# The Parts of a Day

A day has morning,

noon, afternoon, and night.

In the morning the sun rises.

You eat breakfast.

You go to school.

At noon the sun is high above.

In the afternoon the bus

takes you home from school.

After dinner the sun sets

and night falls.

ICE, INC.

OWNED & OPERATED
YAEGER BUS SERVIC
MANKATO, MN

# What Lasts a Day?

What can you do in a day?

You can play outside.

You can build a castle.

Weather often stays for a day.

One day rain falls.

The next day the sun shines.

Celebrations last a day.

You celebrate your birthday.

You can celebrate Earth Day.

Look at your calendar.

What can you celebrate today?

# Glossary

**calendar**—a chart that shows all of the days, weeks, and months in a year

**celebration**—a gathering with activities on a special day

**Earth Day**—a special day for people to help take care of Earth's environment; April 22 is Earth Day

**midnight**—twelve o'clock in the middle of the night

# Read More

**Downing, Johnette**. *Today Is Monday in New York*. Gretna, La.: Pelican Pub. Co., 2011.

**Fujikawa, Gyo**. *Oh, What a Busy Day*. New York: Sterling Pub. Co., 2010.

**Rustad, Martha**. *The Sun*. Out in Space. Mankato, Minn.: Capstone Press, 2009.

# Internet Sites

FactHound offers a safe, fun way to find Internet sites related to this book. All of the sites on FactHound have been researched by our staff.

Here's all you do:

Visit *www.facthound.com*

Type in this code: 9781429675918

 Check out projects, games and lots more at **www.capstonekids.com**

# Index

Word Count: 186
Grade: 1
Early-Intervention Level: 19